This book belongs to

....

Quarto is the authority on a wide range of topics.

Quarto educates, entertains and enriches the lives of
our readers—enthusiasts and lovers of hands-on living.

www.quartoknows.com

© 2018 Quarto Publishing plc

First published in 2018 by QED Publishing,
an imprint of The Quarto Group.
The Old Brewery, 6 Blundell Street,
London N7 9BH, United Kingdom.
T (0)20 7700 6700 F (0)20 7700 8066
www.QuartoKnows.com

A catalogue record for this book is available from the
British Library.

ISBN 978-1-91241-387-4

Based on the original story by Caroline Castle and
Daniel Howarth
Author of adapted text: Katie Woolley
Series Editor: Joyce Bentley
Series Designer: Sarah Peden

Manufactured in Dongguan, China TL042018

9 8 7 6 5 4 3 2 1

FSC
www.fsc.org

MIX
Paper from
responsible sources
FSC® C104723

Reading
Gems

Big
and
FUZZY

QED

On the snow was a house.

It was an igloo!

It was Sira and Ivik's igloo house.

They set off to fish.

Someone saw them.

Sira fished and fished.
Ivik went to sleep.

But someone big and fuzzy
was watching them.

Sira got a fish!

Ivik gave the fish away.

Sira got lots and lots of fish.

Ivik gave them away.

Sira and Ivik set off back home.

But where were all the fish?

15

The wind howled
and howled.

Sira and Ivik walked
and walked.

They got lost
in the snow.

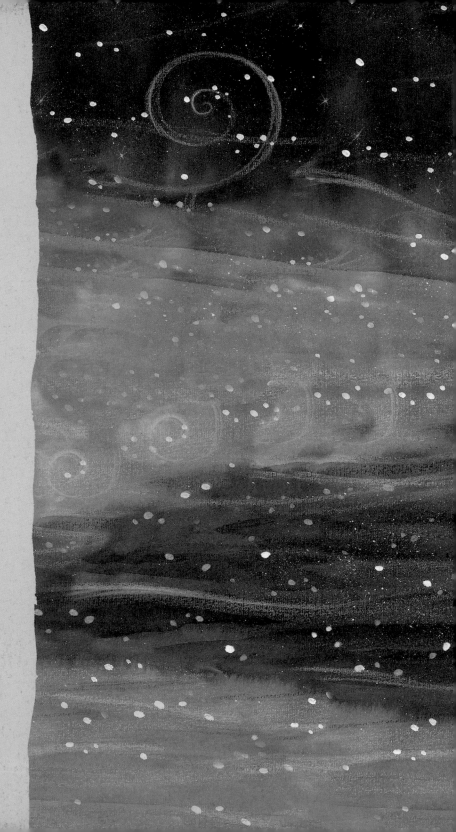

Sira saw a cave. Sira and Ivik went to sleep.

A fuzzy bear went into the cave.

The bear took Sira
and Ivik back to
the igloo house.

On the snow was a fish!

We are home.

Fish!

23

Story Words

bear

cave

fish

igloo

Ivik

lost

Sira

sleep

snow

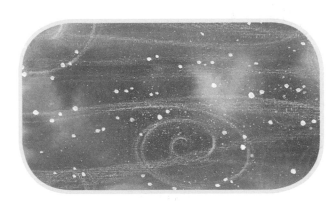

wind

Let's Talk About Big and Fuzzy

Look at the book cover.

Who is on the front of the book?

How can you tell the story is set in a cold place?

What do you like to do when it's snowing?

In the story, Sira is fishing for food in the snow.

What kind of food do you like to eat?

What food do you not like?

In the story, someone is always watching Sira and Ivik.

Is this character mean or kind?

What clues do you see in the pictures to give you the answer?

What other animals live on the ice or snow of the Arctic?

How do the animals keep warm?

How do Ivik and Sira keep warm in the snow?

Did you like the story?

Who was your favourite character?

Fun and Games

Can you match the words to the pictures?

sleep   bear   walk   wind

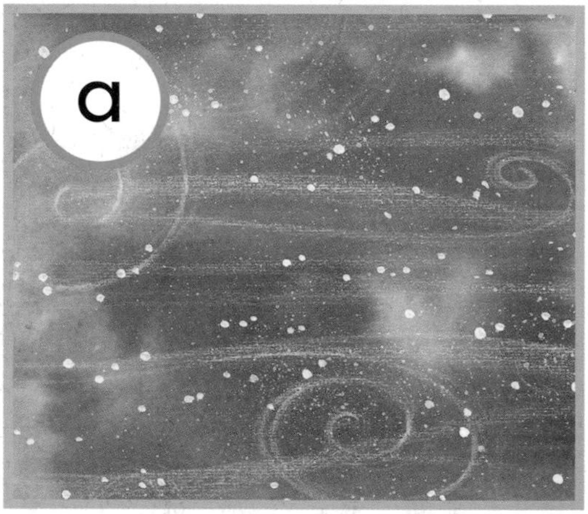

a

b

c

d

Answers: a: wind; b: bear; c: sleep; d: walk.

Look at the pictures. What are they?
What letter sound does each word begin
with? Follow the trails to see if you are right!

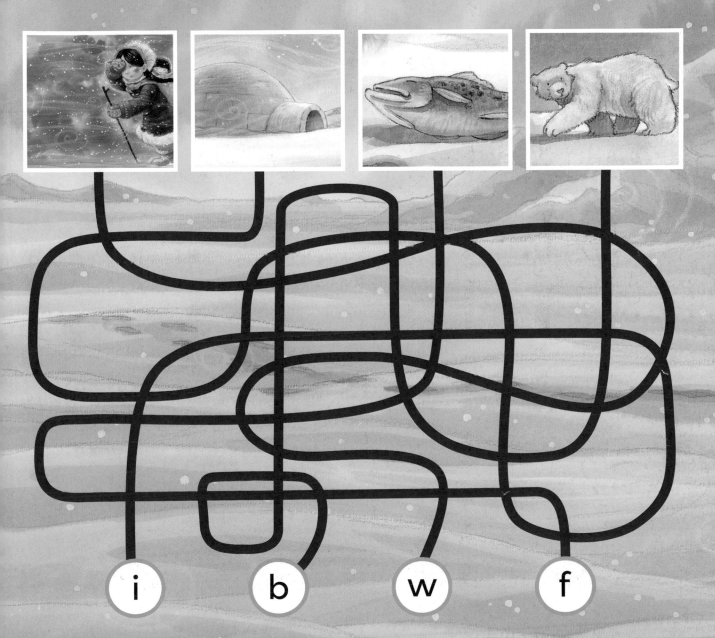

Answers: walk; igloo; fish and bear.

Your Turn

Now that you have read the story,
have a go at telling it in your own words.
Use the pictures below to help you.

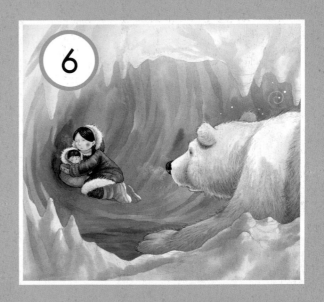

GET TO KNOW READING GEMS

Reading Gems is a series of books that has been written for children who are learning to read. The books have been created in consultation with a literacy specialist.

The books fit into four levels, with each level getting more challenging as a child's confidence and reading ability grows. The simple text and fun illustrations provide gradual, structured practice of reading. Most importantly, these books are good stories that are fun to read!

Level 1 is for children who are taking their first steps into reading. Story themes and subjects are familiar to young children, and there is lots of repetition to build reading confidence.

Level 2 is for children who have taken their first reading steps and are becoming readers. Story themes are still familiar but sentences are a bit longer, as children begin to tackle more challenging vocabulary.

Level 3 is for children who are developing as readers. Stories and subjects are varied, and more descriptive words are introduced.

Level 4 is for readers who are rapidly growing in reading confidence and independence. There is less repetition on the page, broader themes are explored and plot lines straddle multiple pages.

Big and Fuzzy is all about a brother and sister who get lost in the snow. It explores the theme of helping others.

Level 2

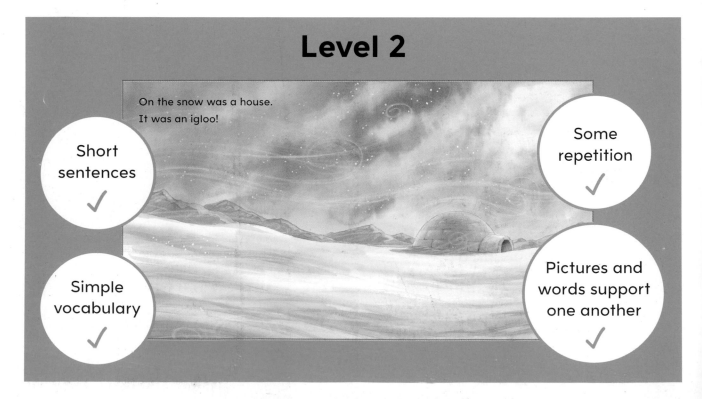

On the snow was a house.
It was an igloo!

Short sentences ✓

Some repetition ✓

Simple vocabulary ✓

Pictures and words support one another ✓